CAN YOU SEE WHAT I SEE?
·T·O·Y·S·
READ-AND-SEEK

WALTER WICK

Cartwheel BOOKS® SCHOLASTIC INC.

New York Toronto London Auckland Sydney
Mexico City New Delhi Hong Kong Buenos Aires

Text copyright © 2008 by Walter Wick.
"String Game," "Magic Mirror," "Bump, Bump, Bump!," "Alphabet Maze," and "See-Through" from *Can You See What I See?* © 2002 by Walter Wick; "Rise and Shine," "Bedtime," "Dreamtime," "Magical Moon," and "Thirteen O'clock" from *Can You See What I See? Dream Machine* © 2003 by Walter Wick; "Dino Diorama" and "Plush Passions" from *Can You See What I See? Cool Collections* © 2004 by Walter Wick.

Library of Congress Cataloging-in-Publication Data
Wick, Walter.
Can you see what I see? : toys read-and-seek / Walter Wick.
p. cm.
ISBN 0-439-86228-0
1. Picture puzzles—Juvenile literature. I. Title.
GV1507.P47W5143 2008
793.73—dc22   2007037842

ISBN-13: 978-0-439-86228-8
ISBN-10: 0-439-86228-0

10 9 8 7 6 5 4 3 2   8 9 10 11 12/0

Printed in the U.S.A. • First printing, May 2008

Dear Reader,

Read the words and find the hidden objects. For an extra challenge, cover the picture clues at the bottom of each page with your hand.

Have fun!

Walter Wick

Can you see

a hat,

2 cats,

and 2 dogs?

Can you see

2 starfish,

a shark,

and 2 frogs?

Can you see

a horse,

and a dog

with a bone?

Can you see

a spider,

a boat,

and a phone?

Can you see

a chicken,

a bunny,

a bell?

Can you see

an owl,

a fork,

and a shell?

GOLFER McCADDIE

GAME of

SCARE

THE
MIRROR
ON THIS
MAGIC MIRROR
TRANSFORMED INTO PICTURES BY
McLOUGHLIN BROS.

6 1
3
4 2 5

Castle Plates

The Butler's Daughter

GAME
EDY

DIRECTIONS FOR THE AMERICAN GAME.

Two, three or four persons can play.
The implements are the same as in the preceding game.
Each player takes six Winks, one Tiddledy, and a number of counters.
Each distributes seven counters to form a pool.
One player acts as leader, takes charge of the pool and makes all payments from it. The pool grows more or less according to the play.
The Wink-pot is placed in the center of the table.
The object is to jump as many Winks into the Wink-pot as possible.
Each plays in turn to the left, the one to lead being decided by lot.
Each player places his Winks at any distance from the Wink-pot he pleases, and jumps his six

Can you see

a baseball,

a hot dog,

a house?

Can you see

a sea horse,

a chimp,

and a mouse?

Can you see

2 chickens,

2 tigers,

and a dragon?

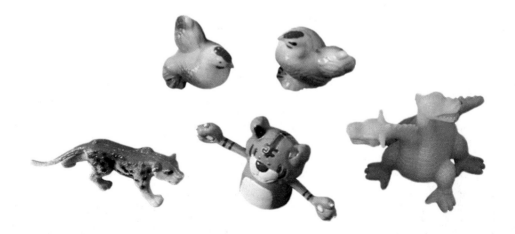

Can you see

a tub,

a clock,

and a wagon?

Can you see

a green bottle and

a blue kangaroo?

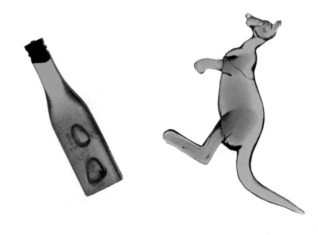

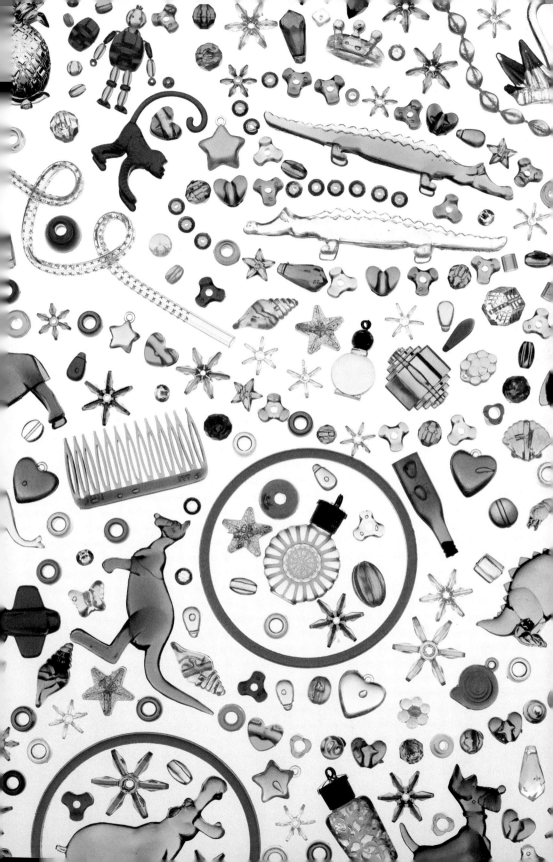

Can you see

a pumpkin,

a moon,

and a shoe?

baseball

bell

boat

bottle

bunny

cats

chicken

chickens

chimp

clock

dog with a bone

dogs

dragon

fork

frogs

hat

horse

hot dog

house

kangaroo

moon

mouse

owl

phone

pumpkin

sea horse

shark

shell

shoe

spider

starfish

tigers

tub

wagon